SIXTY YEARS OF A.1. SERVICE

GEORGE HEANEY

were purchased in
the

the ca...
top of Glasgow Street, ...
shortly after delivery and was
owned by Ian Duff of the same
town.
Ian Maclean

Front cover; Amongst the shoals of Cravens, Park Royal and Weymann bodied buses obtained from London Transport in the 1950s and 1960s, there were also a few with Metro-Cammell bodywork. Leyland Titan KGU 55 was one which was used in service by Brown from 1967 until 1970, and thereafter broken up for spares over the next three years. This April 1970 view shows it at Parkhouse road stance in Ardrossan with Alexander bodied Daimler Fleetlines PAG 765H and PAG 766H in the background; these buses had just been delivered to Ian Duff a few weeks earlier.
Harry Hay

Back cover upper; In 1950 Andrew Hunter took delivery of DCS 616, a Daimler CVD6 with 35 seat coachwork by Irvine of Salsburgh, a firm better known in recent years as the operator of the bus service between Airdrie and Shotts. After eight years service, DCS 616 was rebodied with a Massey 61-seat rear entrance double deck body as shown in this August 1976 photograph at Stevenston Cross. It was sold for preservation later that year but has recently been operating as an open top bus on loan to Midland Scottish for a tourist service in Stirling.
Harry Hay

Back cover lower; Several new Leyland Olympian double deck buses were purchased by various members in 1989, including F149 XCS which is one of four all-Leyland products. This bus is owned by Duff's share based at Parkhouse Garage, Ardrossan and when new it entered service with registration F523 WSJ but due to an administrative error it had to have that number replaced by its current mark. This May 1990 photograph shows it in Manse Street, Saltcoats.
G. M. Heaney

Contents

Foreword	3
The Background	5
The Company	7
Fleet numbers	13
The Vehicles	14
The 1991 Fleet	43
Route Map	48

Large numbers of former London Transport RT class buses joined the A1 fleet during the 1950s and 1960s; JXN 347, a Park Royal bodied example was bought by Hunter of Kilmarnock in November 1958. It was photographed quite soon after this in Irvine High Street - now subject to a bus priority arrangement.
George Waugh collection.

Acknowledgements

THIS BOOK COULD NOT have been produced without a great deal of assistance which has been given to the author over a number of years by many of the A1 Service owners, both past and present, together with drivers, conductors and others who have worked for the company. Assistance has also been given over the years by the PSV Circle and many of its members, together with other individuals and organisations too numerous to list here. The work of those who supplied the photographs which illustrate this book is also appreciated.

The author is continuing to work towards a fully detailed history of the company, its services and vehicles. To this end any reader who has memories, records or particularly old photographs relating to A1 is invited to contact either the author or the company's office at Parkhouse Road, Ardrossan.

First published 1991
ISBN 0 946265 16 X
© Bus Enthusiast Publishing Company, 1991
Typeset in Times and Helvetica
Electronic page makeup by Jeremy Scott
Printed by Howie and Seath, Edinburgh

Published by
Bus Enthusiast Publishing Company
5 Hallcroft Close, Ratho, Newbridge
Midlothian EH28 8SD
Bus Enthusiast is an imprint of
Arthur Southern Ltd.

Foreword

IT IS FITTING that in its sixtieth official year of existence the A.1. bus service, Ayrshire Bus Owners (A.1.Service) Limited, to use the full legal title, is having some of its interesting history commemorated in this book.

There has always been a high level of interest in the company from both transport enthusiasts and professionals due in the main to the peculiar organisation of the company and its varied fleet of buses. Although it is rightly said that every organisation is a mystery to the outsider many seem to have some idea how the company works with the various members trading under one name yet, still existing as separate businesses in their own right.

In the past many articles about the company have appeared in the trade and enthusiast press. There was even an article in the Scots Magazine in November 1977 entitled "The Friendly Buses"; at times working from the other side I have felt that the opposite statement would have been more truthful! However, nothing appearing in print thus far has been as comprehensive as the information, history, illustrations and background contained in this book put together in a most thorough manner by George Heaney. George is well known to most of the directors and is looked upon as the company's unofficial historian because of the time he has spent studying and researching its history.

The company hopes that this commemorative book will provide its readers whether customers, transport enthusiasts or transport professionals with some insight into the history of the company.

D.E.D. Blades,
General Manager

The number of owners has reduced steadily over the years. In 1982 there were thirteen, they were all photographed on the occasion of James J. Murray retiring. The photograph shows (from left to right): James McKinnon; John McMenemy; John Hunter; William J. Meney; James Hunter; James D. McMenemy; James J. Murray; James C. Stewart; Nan Murray; Edward Docherty; Ian M. Duff; John Stewart; George L. Stewart; Robert Meney; Claude Dunn; Tom A. Hill (behind); Mary Hunter; Gordon R. Steele; James A. Brown.
Ron Vavasour

Having been tried by various members, including Docherty, Hill, and Meney, during the summer months of 1984, this Volvo Citybus demonstrator was acquired by Docherty in February 1985. A308 RSU has a distinctive style of East Lancs coachwork and was caught by the camera when negotiating Saltcoats war memorial roundabout; the supermarket in the background has been built on the site of the church which features in many photographs of buses in Saltcoats.
G. M. Heaney

The Background

THE HISTORY OF the Ayrshire Bus Owners (A1 Service) Ltd company can be traced back to the early years of this century when most of the public transport in and between the towns of North Ayrshire was provided by horse-drawn wagonettes. Typically, these carriages held about a dozen passengers, were open to the elements and plied between many of the towns, such as Ardrossan and Saltcoats. Because of the practice of their drivers to shout "Here you are for Ardrossan" (or elsewhere) these carriages became popularly known as "here-y'ares". Some of the operators of these here-y'ares, such as the Murray brothers of Saltcoats, later graduated to charabancs and buses, and eventually became A1 members.

The first steps away from the here-y'are local public transport came around the time of the First World War when the earliest motor buses began to appear in the area. At first they were mainly on chassis designed as lorries and held up to about twenty people on transverse wooden seats, giving rise to the name

of "toast racks". After the War ended large numbers of suitable chassis became available from the War Department (including American made vehicles) and as a result the number of bus operators mushroomed. In the area bounded by Ayr, Kilmarnock and Largs there were about sixty small companies running buses by the early 1920s. In addition to these operators the Scottish General Transport Company (a predecessor of Western Scottish) had commenced operations in the district with a service from the Eglinton Arms Hotel, Ardrossan to Kilmarnock, together with a summer-only charabanc service from Saltcoats War Memorial to Largs. Most of the smaller outfits competed with the "Transport" by operating for varying lengths on the Kilmarnock to Ardrossan route e.g. Saltcoats to Stevenston or Irvine to Kilmarnock. A minority covered other routes such as Irvine to Ayr, Saltcoats to Largs, Kilmarnock to Southook.

By 1924 at least forty operators had been attracted to provide bus services on some section of the

Representative of many of the vehicles which the various owners had when the limited company was formed is this Reo with 20-seat Eaton bodywork. GE 4003 was new in March 1929 and supplied to Mrs Ellen Reid of Saltcoats by a Glasgow dealer, Sharkey Brown. It is likely that this bus remained in the fleet until the mid-1930s when larger vehicles were bought by Reid.
R. L. Grieves collection

Ardrossan to Kilmarnock route, with the Scottish General being the only one attempting to run to a timetable. Most of the other companies could not sensibly do so as they only had one or two buses each. In that year Scottish General moved its headquarters from Bothwell to a new bus station in Kilmarnock and, having done so, proceeded to develop a service network radiating from that town to other centres in Ayrshire. In these circumstances and with rare foresight, it became apparent to the small operators that mutual support and co-operation was the only alternative to being swallowed up or run off the road by the major company. It

was therefore decided in 1925 to send delegates from Ayrshire to investigate the workings of the Lanarkshire Bus Owners Association, which had already been in operation for some time providing services between Newmains and Glasgow.

As a result of the delegates' findings, steps were taken in the autumn of 1925 to set up the Ayrshire Bus Owners Association which was to be permitted to use the same operating title of "A1 Service" which their counterparts in Lanarkshire had been using. Immediately after the New Year holiday at the beginning of 1926 this new association began through running between Ardrossan and Kilmarnock to a set timetable. About the same time another, completely separate, bus owners association was formed under the name of "LS" for Local Service and comprised those operators who had previously confined themselves to running a shuttle service between Stevenston and Saltcoats.

At the outset only about a dozen bus owners joined the A1 Association but this membership very quickly expanded to include not only more owners in the Ardrossan-Kilmarnock corridor but operators on the routes from Kilmarnock to Darvel and Old Cumnock, and from Ardrossan to Largs and Ayr. Within six months membership had increased to nearly forty, and more than sixty owners have been identified as having been members of the association during the following three or four years.

From 1929 to 1931 a certain amount of regrouping took place amongst the bus operators in North Ayrshire. In the Spring of 1929 certain members of both the A1 and LS associations decided to concentrate on the Largs route and resigned from their organisations to form a new association called CCS, or Clyde Coast Service. In 1930 the majority of the remaining A1 members agreed not to compete with Scottish General on any route other than that between Ardrossan and Kilmarnock. This decision, coupled with an A1 ruling that no member should operate more than two buses in the group (apart from Dodds of Troon who had joined A1 in 1926 with three buses) resulted in a further split in the ranks of A1 members, with eight leaving in April 1930 to form the Ayrshire Bus Owners Association AA Service, set up to operate principally between Ayr and Ardrossan. Finally, in May 1931 the remaining members of the LS association applied for A1 membership, and their acceptance with equal rights resulted in A1 beginning to operate on the local services between Ardrossan and Stevenston, in addition to the trunk route between Ardrossan and Kilmarnock, with all the duties being shared by all the members.

The chaotic state of bus operations in the mid 1920s had led to further control on the running of buses being introduced in 1928, albeit on a haphazard basis, through local bye-laws which empowered

James Drysdale of Dreghorn was one of the initial members of the company, but in 1934 this membership lapsed and the share was cancelled without replacement, thus reducing the total number of owners to 21. One of Drysdale's buses was SL1602, a Minerva with full-fronted 25-seat bodywork which was new to Ferguson's of Alloa in September 1931 but which had entered service with A1 less than a year later.
R. L. Grieves collection

magistrates to licence all buses which operated within the local authorities' area. These powers were utilised by a number of authorities in North Ayrshire, including the burghs of Ardrossan, Largs and Saltcoats, and led to annual inspections of the buses and the subsequent allocation of licences to them. Not all authorities undertook this work, and the system was not altogether satisfactory. When regulation of the British bus industry was eventually introduced under the 1930 Road Traffic Act these powers of inspection were vested in the Traffic Commissioners, and operator, vehicle and route licencing were brought into effect. These changes encouraged operator associations such as those in Ayrshire to organise in a more formal way, and on 27 May 1931 a limited company was incorporated under the title of Ayrshire Bus Owners (A1 Service) Ltd to continue the business of the Ayrshire Bus Owners Association A1 Service.

The Company

AT THE FORMATION of the new limited company there were 22 bus owners included in the organisation, and their names are listed on page 13. After a period of such instability in the bus industry it is hardly surprising that a few changes to the initial ownership position took place before a state of equilibrium was reached. The Dreghorn-based business of the Hosie family became the first share in the company to change hands when it passed to Mrs Elizabeth Kerr of Saltcoats, later Ardrossan, in 1933. In 1934 the share of another Dreghorn owner, James Drysdale, was cancelled without replacement after a period of some difficulties, and this reduced the total number of members to 21. After this, no further significant changes in the ownership of the shares in the company took place until after the Second World War.

In 1948 the first two members wishing to retire from the company, Joseph Docherty of Ardrossan and Mrs Margaret Evans (previously Mrs Wilson) of Saltcoats, sold their units

to J. J. Murray and William Townsley respectively, resulting in the latter members becoming the first owners to hold a double share in the company. In the early 1950s several other original owners sold out, but their shares passed into the hands of individuals who had not previously been members. New owners admitted at that time comprised James Brown of Springside (later Dreghorn), John Duff of Ardrossan, James McKinnon of Kilmarnock and Robert Steele of Stevenston, but shortly after this an agreement was reached that shares would only be sold to members' families or to other members, no doubt to guard against the possibility of the company falling into the hands of a competitor. In consequence of this, the number of owners in the company has fallen gradually over the years but the number of double share owners has increased. A complication which has arisen from time to time has been when a double share owner wished to sell; in these circumstances the double share concerned has until now been split be-

CS 258 was an Albion Valiant PV70 with 32-seat sun saloon bodywork built by F. D. Cowieson of St Rollox, Glasgow. It was ordered by member Alistair Macphail of Irvine on 9 February 1934, the chassis left Albion Motors factory on 5 March and the complete vehicle was delivered to Macphail on 30 March, the whole process having taken just seven weeks. It gave its owner good service, lasting until 1957 (albeit with a replacement body) when Macphail's share was acquired by T. & E. Docherty.
Albion Motors

tween two other owners. Although a few single share owners remained, the position was reached in November 1988 that Stewart of Saltcoats wished to sell his share to Robert Meney of the same town, who was already a double owner. The company sanctioned this arrangement and Meney therefore became the first triple share owner; by the summer of 1991 Brown, Docherty and Stewart were also in this position. Ignoring

the role of the company itself as the owner of two minibuses, there were four triple share owners, three double share owners and three single share owners at that time.

At first the registered office of the company was at 17 Eglinton Street, Irvine but on 29 July 1936 this was changed to the bus station, Parkhouse Road, Ardrossan, i.e. when the Parkhouse Road stance came into operation. Prior to this the Ardrossan terminus had been at the top of Glasgow Street, initially on the street but later on ground owned by an adjacent garage. Consideration was also given in the mid-1930s to the purchase of land in Kilmarnock for the construction of a stance but the eventual decision was to take no action at that time. It was only in post-war years that steps were taken to obtain an off-street terminus in Kilmarnock; the first stance was off St Marnock Street, but in 1959 a new A1 bus station was opened in John Dickie Street. In the subsequent redevelopment of Kilmarnock town centre another new bus station was built to replace both the A1 and separate Western SMT facilities, and A1 was allocated two stances and office space in it.

Over the years the original routes have been adapted to serve new developments and the general expansion of the towns along the routes. A feature of this process during the years of bus industry regulation up to the 1980s were the Traffic Commissioners court battles between A1 and Western over the right to serve any new development. Despite this, a network of local routes grew up in Ardrossan, Saltcoats and Stevenston with A1 clearly the major operator in that area. With the designation of Irvine as a New Town incorporating Kilwinning and Dreghorn, further network development was assured in the 1970s. Particularly significant in this respect was the commence-

In 1939 five new AEC Regals were delivered to A1 Service members, four having Pickering bodies and the odd one out bodied by Willowbrook. CS 9453 was one of the Pickering examples and arrived in March 1939. It was owned by Robert Paterson of Ardrossan who entered a partnership three years later with Thomas Hill to form Hill and Paterson, later based in Stevenston and now trading as the Stevenston Motor Co. This bus, which was allocated fleet number 30, lasted until 1954.
Roy Marshall

ment in 1976 of an Irvine-Dreghorn service via the Broomlands bus-only "community route". The 1980 Transport Act freed longer-distance bus services from regulation, permitting the introduction of services between Ayrshire and Glasgow at a time when the parallel rail services were less than reliable and pending electrification. A new operator, Bennett's of

Kilwinning, pioneered these services but A1 quickly responded by starting Ardrossan/Glasgow and Dundonald/Glasgow routes. The 1980 Act was only a prelude to full deregulation of all bus services under the 1985 Transport Act. Since deregulation took effect in October 1986 the A1 Service network has been consolidated to discourage competition, but the most significant development so far took place in July 1990 when two minibus routes were introduced on an experimental basis, one between Ardrossan and Stevenston, and the other within Kilwinning. Several changes were subsequently made to the routes followed by these services, but the decision has been taken to make these operations permanent.

A high frequency has always been maintained on the trunk route between Ardrossan and Kilmarnock. Despite the progressive introduction of higher capacity vehicles it was clearly difficult to reduce the frequency to any significant extent with 21 shares in the company providing at least one vehicle. This no doubt partially explains the relatively good patronage still enjoyed on the route and the absence of time-table leaflets until the 1970s, but also exemplifies the meticulous care which has

had to be taken since the beginning to ensure equality of treatment for all members. Duties have been arranged in such a way that over a period each operator would operate on all routes, although for many years an exception was that the Ardrossan-Kilmarnock route was divided into two with those members at the "Kilmarnock end" operating on the schedule starting and finishing at Kilmarnock while those at the "Ardrossan end" operated a rota of schedules starting and finishing at Ardrossan. A considerable amount of dead mileage was eliminated by this method although operators in the middle of the route, such as McMenemy when based at Kilwinning, still had a considerable amount of non-revenue-earning mileage each morning and evening. For many years each operator retained the fares collected on his own buses except for return and weekly tickets; all return tickets carried an identifying letter and were retained by the conductor on the return journey, an exchange ticket being issued. The appropriate portion of the value of the ticket was then credited to the owner on whose bus the return journey was made. All receipts from the sale of weekly tickets were pooled under this system. Revised arrange-

One of the earliest double deck buses in the A1 Service fleet was this Foden PVD6 believed to have bodywork built by the Scottish Commercial Motor Co. of Townhead in Glasgow; this was actually a firm of motor vehicle dealers and it is not clear which "Scottish Commercial" bodies were merely supplied by the company, rather than built by it. CAG 76 was owned by Andrew Hunter of Dreghorn and in 1955 it was rebodied with a Weymann product from a former Liverpool Corporation Guy Arab. This photograph shows it as it was in 1953, in Glasgow Street, Ardrossan.
Roy Marshall

ments were, however, introduced for the distribution of revenue in 1977.

Crew operation was retained by the company on all routes until well after this had been given up by most other firms. The initial step in the direction of one-person operation was taken in January 1983 when the Ardrossan, Saltcoats and Stevenston local routes were converted to this system. Since then, further phases in this conversion have been implemented, with the result that crew operation is now used only on the Ardrossan-Kilmarnock service during the main part of the day on Mondays to Saturdays.

In 1955 four former Liverpool Corporation Guy Arabs with Weymann bodies entered service with four different members. Their chassis dated from 1943 but the bodies had been built pre-war for use on other vehicles. A fifth example of the type was used by Andrew Hunter to rebody his Foden CAG 76. GKC 249 was owned by John Duff of Ardrossan and was photographed in the St Marnock Street stance in Kilmarnock, shortly before that facility was replaced by the bus station in John Dickie Street.
Ian Maclean

Two of the ex-London Transport Cravens bodied AEC Regents were rebodied during their spell in the A1 Service fleet. One was JXC 192, purchased by Murray in June 1956 and eight years later given the Park Royal body from another ex-London Transport AEC Regent, JXN 203, which had been bought by this member for spares. Platform doors were added at the same time, and in 1970 the bus was sold to another member, Stewart of Saltcoats who continued to operate it for some years.
B. T. Deans

At the 1961 Scottish Motor Show in the Kelvin Hall, Glasgow, Daimler displayed the first Fleetline ordered by a Scottish operator in the shape of a Northern Counties bodied vehicle for Tom Hunter of Kilmarnock, one of a pair which had been called for by that owner. The second of these buses entered service in October 1962 as UCS 763, seen here in Princes Street, Ardrossan.
R. H. G. Simpson

In November 1964 James McKinnon took delivery of a pair of AEC Renowns with the Park Royal forward entrance bodywork usually fitted to this type. At that time McKinnon was another owner running white-roofed buses, but another distinguishing feature of this owner's vehicles was the triangular shaped destination screen. This view of ASD 891B leaving the A1 bus station in John Dickie Street, Kilmarnock, illustrates both of these characteristics.
R. F. Mack

OCS 114R, seen passing Stewart's garage in Boglemart Street, Stevenston, is an Alexander AD-type bodied Daimler Fleetline owned by McKinnon since new in 1976, but actually ordered by a Stoke-on-Trent operator.
John Burnett

Alexander bodied Leyland Atlantean JGA 198N, originally owned by the Greater Glasgow Passenger Transport Executive, was acquired by John Hunter of Kilmarnock in 1985. This March 1989 view in Vernon Street, Saltcoats shows the bus standing on the exact spot occupied by a depot used by former member Murray of Saltcoats; the buildings concerned were demolished about ten years ago to permit the widening of Vernon Street. John Hunter retired in November 1989 and ownership of his share passed to Docherty.
M. Currie

Fleet Numbers

This rear view of Croft bodied AEC Regal BSD 561 and Leyland bodied Leyland Titan PD2 CSD 233 at the Ardrossan stance in June 1950 illustrates the use of fleetnumbers. These numbers were generally applied to the rear of the vehicles within a traditional belt and buckle design which also incorporated the fleetname. BSD 561 belonged to Jonathan Stewart and was numbered 33A at the time of this photograph, while CSD 233 belonged to McMenemy and was numbered 25.
A. B. Cross

IN AUGUST 1931 it was agreed that a fleetnumbering system was to be introduced for all A1 Service vehicles. The system adopted, however, was tailored to the composition of the company with each share or unit allocated two numbers, that being the maximum number of buses which any owner could put out on service at that time. The following table illustrates the original position (see opposite).

When in later years some of the owners began to operate three or more buses, an "A" suffix was added to one of the fleet numbers. For example, for many years Andrew Hunter of Dreghorn ran three buses with fleetnumbers 16, 16A and 17. The use of these fleetnumbers by all A1 owners continued until about 1950, by which time the advent of double share ownership in the fleet had given the system less validity. Although some owners stopped using their allocated fleetnumbers in the 1950s, others continued the practice for another twenty years or so. By 1980, however, use of these numbers had ceased altogether.

In the 1970s an attempt was made to develop a new fleet numbering system based on the registration numbers of the buses whereby efforts were made to get registrations under 100 for all new buses. Difficulties with the local taxation office and the purchase of second-hand buses which did not fit into this system led to problems, and the idea was abandoned after a while, but this explains the high proportion of buses in the fleet with low registration numbers.

Share No.	Directors	Vehicle Nos.
1	Charles Brennan, Ardrossan	1, 44
2	Hugh Carlin, Crosshouse	2, 43
3	Mrs Elizabeth Cunningham, Ardrossan	3, 45
4	Edward Docherty & Son, Stevenston	4, 5
5	Joseph Docherty, Ardrossan	6, 7
6	James Drysdale, Dreghorn	8, 9
7	William Hill, Dreghorn	10, 11
8	Robert Hosie, Dreghorn	12, 14
9	Andrew Hunter, Springside	16, 17
10	Thomas Hunter, Kilmarnock	18, 19
11	Alexander Macphail, Irvine	20, 21
12	Robert Meney, Kilwinning	22, 23
13	James Murray, Saltcoats	15, 24
14	James McMenemy, Kilwinning	25, 26
15	Mrs Ellen Reid, Saltcoats	27, 28
16	William Roy, Ardrossan	29, 30
17	John Stewart, Saltcoats	31, 32
18	Jonathan Stewart, Saltcoats	33, 34
19	William Stewart, Saltcoats	35, 36
20	William Townsley, Saltcoats	37, 38
21	Mrs Margaret Wilson, Saltcoats	39, 40
22	Nathaniel Young, Galston	41, 42

The Vehicles

When the limited company was established the A1 Service fleet included vehicles of many different makes, such as Albion, Bean, Commer, Dennis, Gilford, Leyland, Morris Commercial, Reo, Thornycroft and W & G, all fitted with a wide variety of bodywork, seating from 14 to 26 passengers. Although the standard livery of blue with white and maroon had been adopted in the latter days of the earlier Association, not all buses had been painted into these colours by May 1931; up to two years later the Director's Committee still had occasion to reprimand certain members about their failure to paint their buses into the company colours. Lettering on the vehicles varied from "The A1 Service" to "A1 Service" and less usually "A1 Service Ltd". At first no fleetnumbers were allocated, but a system for this was introduced within a few months of the company being formed.

Although a mixed bag of new and second-hand vehicles arrived in 1931 and 1932, the later part of 1933 saw the delivery of the first examples of what was to become the most common type of A1 bus during the rest of the 1930s — the Albion Victor with bodywork usually built by the Lanarkshire firms of Pickering or Stewart. Other types such as Bedford and Dennis added variety but by the late 1930s AEC Regals, Albion Valkyries and several types of Leyland had been purchased by members. New buses were the order of the day during this period, and to ensure equality amongst the members, strict controls were set on the maximum size of vehicle which could be used on the services. Progressively the maximum seating capacity was increased from the original limit of 26, until 39-seat vehicles were permitted from 1939 onwards in an effort to ensure adequate capacity during the Second World War with the possibility of a depleted fleet strength.

The war years were a difficult period for the A1 Service with several vehicles requisitioned by the authorities and the regular supply of new buses no longer available. In the light of these difficulties the com-

In 1959 Glasgow Corporation Transport ordered 140 Leyland Titan PD3s with Alexander forward entrance bodywork for its tramway replacement programme. A couple of extra vehicles were built to the same specification and one of these was purchased by Docherty from Millburn Motors dealer stock in March 1962. It was registered TSD 285 and was one of the buses which Docherty ran for several years with a white, rather than blue, roof but this had been brought into line with company policy when this photograph was taken at the level crossing in Princes Street, Ardrossan. This bus is still owned although its registration was transferred to a new Volvo Citybus in 1985.
A. J. Douglas

pany rule requiring the purchase of new buses only was waived and in the ensuing years a number of second-hand purchases were made. By 1942 some of the pressure on the ageing fleet was relieved by the allocation of a few Bedford OWB utility buses to these members most in need of new stock; these buses were generally disliked and were replaced as soon as possible after the war ended. Perhaps the most notable development during the war years, however, was the acquisition of the first double deck bus in the fleet. Mrs Cunningham, of Ardrossan, had the distinction of being the first member with such a vehicle — a former Western SMT Leyland Titan TD2 — but it was only used in service for a day or two before being withdrawn as the company rules had not actually been changed in time to permit the use of this bus. It was not long after this, though, that double deck buses were given official blessing and began to feature increasingly in the fleet.

In the immediate post-war years the demand for public transport was growing and investment in new stock was urgently required if the A1 Service was to be in a position to meet the increasing requirements. Between 1946 and 1949 approximately 30 new buses were shared between virtually all of the members comprising not only AEC Regals and Albion Valkyries with Croft or Pickering bodies, but also Crossley, Foden and Leyland double deck buses owned by Andrew Hunter, J. J. Murray, William Townsley, H. & J. Carlin and Mrs McMenemy. With the introduction of these new double deckers most of the other owners were persuaded that this type of bus should be used on the services, and the early 1950s consequently saw a flood of second-hand double deck buses entering the fleet from a wide range of sources. One particularly interesting specimen bought at that time by Kerr and Linney of Ardrossan was a Metro-Cammell bodied Daimler COG6 built at the start of the war for export to Johannesburg but diverted to Birmingham City Transport instead.

The fortunes of A1 Service and its members took a significant turn for the better when London Transport decided in 1956 to sell 120 AEC Regents with non-standard Cravens bodywork which were only eight years old. No less than 25 of these bargains were snapped up by A1 Service members, and as a result the character of the fleet had changed considerably by the end of 1957.

The 1940 Fleet

On 26 June 1940 the Regional Transport Commissioner for the Ministry of Transport requested details of all public service vehicles owned by A1 Service members, in connection with various wartime requirements. Particulars of the following vehicles were supplied by the company, giving a good basis for a summary of the fleet at that time. The fleet numbers do, of course, indicate the owner, see page 13.

Fleet No.	Reg'n no.	Chassis Type	Bodybuilder	Seating capacity
1	CS 3278	Albion Victor PK115	Stewart	26
2	CS 5438	Albion Victor PK115	Pickering	32
3	CS 510	Dennis Lancet I		32
4	CS 5463	Albion Victor PK115	Pickering	32
5	AAG 178	Albion Valkyrie CX9	Pickering	39
6	CS 9514	Albion Victor PK115	Stewart	32
7	CS 6142	Albion Victor PK115	Stewart	32
10	CS 3477	Albion Victor PK115	Pickering	32
11	CS 7985	Albion Valkyrie CX9	Pickering	36
12	CS 9571	Albion Victor PK115	Pickering	32
14	CS 5861	Albion Victor PK115		32
15	CS 9157	Leyland Tiger TS8	Pickering	37
16	CS 8131	Albion Victor PK115	Pickering	32
17	CS 3905	Tilling Stevens Express	Stewart	32
18	CS 2683	Albion Victor PK115	Pickering	32
19	CS 5480	Leyland Lion LT7	Pickering	35
20	CS 258	Albion Valiant PV70	Cowieson	32
21	CS 9804	Albion Valkyrie CX9	Duple	39
22	CS 6472	Leyland Lion LT7	Stewart	32
23	CS 5894	Leyland Lion LT7	Stewart	32
24	CS 3474	Albion Victor PK115		30
25	US 8249	Albion Victor PK115	Cowieson	30
26	CS 8775	Leyland Cheetah LZ2	Pickering	37
27	CS 3637	Dennis Lancet I	Dennis	32
28	CS 2189	Dennis Lancet I		32
29	CS 4238	Leyland Cub SKPZ2		30
30	CS 9453	AEC Regal	Pickering	37
31	CS 9693	AEC Regal	Pickering	37
32	CS 3895	Albion Victor PH115	Cowieson	26
33	CS 9694	AEC Regal	Pickering	37
34	CS 4012	Bedford WTB	Duple	25
35	CS 9695	AEC Regal	Pickering	37
36	CS 4013	Bedford WTB	Duple	25
37	CS 9421	AEC Regal II	Willowbrook	35
38	CS 5303	Leyland Lion LT7	Waveney	36
39	CS 4039	Albion Victor PK115		30
40	CS 8016	Albion Valkyrie CX9	Pickering	32
41	CS 9841	Leyland Lion LT8	Pickering	37
42	CS 7556	Albion Victor PK115	Pickering	32
43	AAG 652	Albion Valkyrie CX9	Pickering	39
44	CS 4801	Bedford WTB	Duple	26
45	CS 4040	Bedford WTB	Duple	25

Notes
CS 510 and CS 2189 may have had Dennis bodywork. CS 4039 may have had Barnaby bodywork.
The bodybuilders for CS 3474, CS 4238 and CS 5861 are not known.

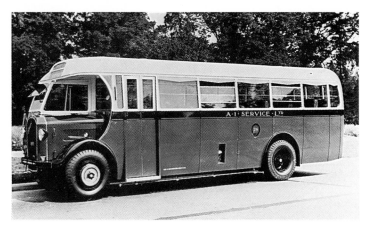

Dennis was another popular make in the A1 Service during the pre-war years, with about a dozen buses of this type having been used by various members at that time. Mrs Ellen Reid of Saltcoats purchased two Dennis Lancets in the mid-1930s, the first of which was delivered in autumn 1935 as CS 2189, shown here. Reid's share was allocated fleetnumbers 27 and 28, and the latter number is clearly visible within the garter on the side panels. In 1967 T. & E. Docherty of Irvine acquired Reid's unit.
Dennis

GLASGOW STREET, ARDROSSAN.

CS4801 was a Duple bodied Bedford WTB supplied new to Charles Brennan of Ardrossan in December 1936 and its fleetnumber 44 can just be made out in this view of Glasgow Street, Ardrossan in 1937. By 1941 this bus had passed to OK Motor Service of Bishop Auckland in County Durham, but it ended its days as a mobile shop in the 1950s. The battery powered bread delivery van of Morrison's Bakery in Stevenston is also noteworthy.
George Waugh collection

Further second-hand double deckers continued to arrive during the remainder of the 1950s and towards the end of that decade it was agreed that only double deckers should be used on the services. This decision not only led to the disappearance of the last single deck buses at that time, but also sounded the death knell for coach operation for most of the members who had purchased a few vehicles of this type during the 1950s and operated them in a cream and maroon "A1 coach livery". Apart from Young Brothers who had always maintained a coach fleet separate from their A1 operation, the only two owners who continued with coaches to any extent were T. & E. Docherty, and James Brown of Dreghorn. In more recent years, others have returned to coach operation.

About the end of 1961 a ruling was introduced within the company that no member could purchase a vehicle for use on the services, over five years old. This even applied to sales between members, and again led to the appearance of new double deck buses from 1962 onwards. Purchases at that time included Northern Counties bodied Daimler Fleetlines for Tom Hunter (including Scotland's first example of this rear-engined type) and more traditional AEC, Daimler and Leyland front engined buses. The ruling about age of vehicles was, however, soon relaxed to allow a limited number of second-hand purchases, and it was not long before substantial quantities of surplus London Transport AEC Regents and Leyland Titans had joined the ranks, in addition to other types.

The last traditional-style double decker to be bought new was a 1965 Leyland Titan PD2A with Massey bodywork supplied to McMenemy, and during the next ten years all new buses were either Daimler Fleetlines or Leyland Atlanteans, albeit with a variety of bodywork styles by Alexander, Massey, Northern Counties and Park Royal. Advantage was taken of ordering in bulk at this time with, for example, three Atlanteans and five Fleetlines with similar Alexander bodies taken in 1973. Two other types of new bus which were favoured in the later 1970s were the front engined Volvo Ailsa, produced half way along the Ardrossan-Kilmarnock route in the former Irvine Royal Ordnance Factory premises, and the Dennis Dominator with East Lancs bodywork. With regular deliveries of new buses throughout the

The A1 Service fleet contained comparatively few Leylands in the 1930s but Robert Meney, based initially in Kilwinning but later at Ardrossan, operated two Leyland Lion LT7s with bodywork by Stewart of Wishaw. The first of them was CS 5894 delivered in 1937, and it is seen here at Parkhouse Road, Ardrossan not long before it was withdrawn in October 1954.
Roy Marshall

CS 9571 was the last of a substantial number of Albion Victor PK 115 models purchased by A1 Service members during the 1930s. It had 32-seat bodywork by R. Y. Pickering of Motherwell and entered service in March 1939, having been ordered by Mrs Elizabeth Kerr of Ardrossan. In the same year the name of James Linney was added to the ownership of this share in the company, and Kerr & Linney continued to be an owner until 1968 when the share was sold to Duff. Kerr & Linney's vehicles were kept at Central Garage, Ardrossan, premises now used by McMenemy.
A. B. Cross

With the onset of the Second World War larger single deck buses were permitted into the fleet, with up to 39 seats. One of the first vehicles of this capacity was ACS 323, an Albion Valkyrie CX9 with Duple bodywork supplied to Robert Brennan of Ardrossan in October 1940. Seen here in Irvine High Street bound for Kilmarnock, this bus ended its days as a furniture van with a firm based in the latter town. Brennan's share in the A1 Service passed to McKinnon of Kilmarnock in September 1953.
R. L. Grieves collection

This Duple bodied Bedford OWB photographed at Parkhouse Road was supplied new to Mrs Elizabeth Cunningham in November 1945. Six other Bedfords of this type were operated by A1 Service members during the Second World War, but had the more utilitarian style of bodywork associated with these buses, including wooden slatted seats. In November 1952, six months before this photograph was taken, Mrs Cunningham sold her share to R. B. Steele of Stevenston whose son is still an owner.
Roy Marshall

1970s, fewer second-hand vehicles were acquired but those that did arrive added variety to the fleet.

With the opportunity to provide a service along the Broomlands community route in Irvine in 1976 came pressure from Irvine Development Corporation to use single deck vehicles on it, as these were perceived to be environmentally more acceptable. T. & E. Docherty agreed to pioneer this new route using single deck buses and consequently purchased a Leyland Leopard with Duple Dominant coach shell/bus seats body, and an ex-London Transport AEC Swift. When the Broomlands service was incorporated into the main duty cycle for all members a few years later, these buses were effectively displaced to other routes, but their presence in the fleet signalled a change in company policy regarding vehicles

whereby a limited number of single deck buses could again be operated. The result of this decision was that from 1980 onwards a small number of Leyland and Volvo saloons entered service. The majority of vehicles bought in the 1980s, however, continued to be double deckers. The popular choices now were the Leyland Olympian and the Volvo Citybus, supplemented by used additions such as former London Transport Fleetlines, Leyland Olympians from the West Yorkshire Passenger Transport Executive fleet, and the complete batch of five experimental Ailsas supplied to Maidstone & District in 1975 which were acquired by the Stevenston Motor Co. and T. & J. Hunter of Kilmarnock.

The 1990s have started off in fine style, insofar as variety in the fleet is concerned. The decision to

introduce minibus operation on an experimental basis resulted in the purchase of a pair of Iveco Daily buses with Phoenix bodywork which are a far cry from the previous generation of 25 seat buses used in A1 Service. The Leyland National also returned to the fleet in 1990 after an absence of some years with the purchase by Edward Docherty of a MkI example from Blackpool Transport. More Ailsas also arrived in 1990 in the shape of no less than seven early models from the Tayside fleet. In 1991 the award of school transport contracts in the Kilmarnock area which had previously been operated by Western Scottish led to an expansion of the fleet with Metro-Cammell or Park Royal bodied Fleetlines from West Midlands Travel being acquired for this work, notably by McKinnon.

April 1946 saw the delivery of BAG 238, the first of a pair of Albion Valkyrie CX13s with Pickering 35-seat bodywork taken by Thomas Docherty of Ardrossan. The maroon flashes visible on the sides in this official view barely disguise the rather utilitarian lines of the body. Together with sister BAG 237, this bus passed to Duff when Docherty's share was sold in 1951, but it spent its last years as a caravan with Cody's Circus.
Albion Motors

BAG 418 was one of no fewer than 13 AEC Regals purchased in 1946-47 with bodywork by Croft of Gallowgate in Glasgow, more recently well-known as a Ford dealer. This bus was delivered in July 1946 to Hill and Paterson of Stevenston and clearly illustrates the striped radiator and silver star which distinguished vehicles belonging to that owner for many years. The photograph was taken at the War Memorial end of Manse Street, Saltcoats — the belisha beacon and associated road markings are noteworthy.
A. B. Cross

Throughout the history of the company, some owners have attempted to personalise their buses. In the late 1940s, at least, many vehicles carried the name of the individual owner inside, either above the door or on the front bulkhead. However, this practice fell into disuse despite a later attempt by T. & E. Docherty to revive it by painting their name on the staircases of some of their vehicles. In more recent times some owners have, nevertheless, put their names on their buses by advertising other facets of their business, such as Stewart's Travel Centre and Steele's welding services, in the conventional positions for adverts. Although the blue, white and maroon livery was adopted at an early date many owners have applied these colours in a sufficiently distinctive

way to allow knowledgeable onlookers to identify the owner concerned. Thus, while blue roofs were the norm for double deck buses, for some years McKinnon continued the practice followed by Townsley and painted the roofs of his double deck buses white, and added attractive white lining out and a "Travel A1" inscription on the rear lower panel. For many years Murray's buses carried a "Travel by bus" legend in a similar position. In 1962 Docherty also adopted white roofs but about four years later the other members decided that all buses should be given blue roofs. Other touches of individuality have included variation in the number and placing of red bands used by several members, and the application of blue and maroon vertical stripes to the radiators of Hill

and Paterson's buses until the advent of rear engines put an end to this. As a reminder of the ornamental brasswork common on earlier A1 bus radiators, Hill and Paterson's buses also carried a silver star on the radiator and some of the successor Stevenston Motor Company buses still carry this on the front today. Bulk purchase of new buses in the 1970s resulted in fewer livery variations in the fleet as a whole and another factor which has contributed to this has been the reduced use made of maroon as an economy measure, to the extent that Steele is unfortunately the only owner now applying this colour to all of his vehicles. Despite this, no other bus company comes to mind that has had quite the same variety of types and appearance of vehicles as the A1 Service.

BSD 904 was one of a pair of Croft bodied Albion Valkyries delivered in November 1946. It was photographed in Queen Street, Edinburgh while on a private hire some years later, by which time it had been repainted into the A1 coach livery. This bus was initially owned by Hugh Cheyne, who by 1947 was the registered holder of the Dreghorn-based share of Mrs Hill, but in 1950 this share was sold to James Brown, of Springside and this bus was one of the vehicles transferred to the new owner.
A. T. Smith

The bodywork on this Crossley DD42 was another product labelled as Scottish Commercial, but it was possibly built by Charles H. Roe, of Leeds. In either case, CCS 800 was supplied to H. & J. Carlin of Crosshouse in March 1949, but in the following year Carlin's share in the company was sold to Hunter of Kilmarnock, and this bus passed into the ownership of Murray of Saltcoats who retained it until 1959. Stevenston Cross is the location of this 1953 view.
Roy Marshall

Possibly one of the best known buses to have been in the A1 Service fleet is NTF 9, a 1951 Leyland Titan PD2 with Leyland 56-seat bodywork. This bus was originally a Leyland demonstrator but was acquired by T. & E. Docherty in time for that owner's return to membership of A1 in 1957, after an absence of a few years. Although it has not been used in regular passenger service for many years it has been called on to perform from time to time, as in July 1984 when a vintage bus service was provided by A1 Service, AA Motors and Western SMT between Irvine Cross and Irvine Harbour in connection with the Irvine Harbour Festival.
G. M. Heaney

In October 1961 the business of J. Laurie & Co. (Chieftain), Hamilton was absorbed by Central S.M.T., and at that time Chieftain was in the vanguard of Scottish bus operators in having ordered two rear engined buses in the shape of Leyland Atlanteans. When Central sold these buses in 1969 one of them, 60 AVA, passed to A1 Service member R. B. Steele. The Metro-Cammell bodywork was typical of the earliest rear engined double deck buses in its rather square appearance. It lasted in the A1 fleet until 1974.
I. MacGregor

During the 1950s several owners had coaches or single deck buses painted in a cream and maroon livery, occasionally with a little blue, as a variant of the normal bus fleet colours. Some of these vehicles were frequently used on the services when circumstances required it and the example illustrated was no exception. CSD 192 was a Plaxton bodied Dennis Lancet of 1949 owned by William Stewart and Sons, of Stevenston. It is seen in Boglemart Street in that town, outside the depot shared for many years by two units, William Stewart/J. C. Stewart and Jonathan Stewart/ Claude Dunn, but originally built by Joseph Docherty when his share in the company was based in Stevenston.
R. F. Mack

In the early 1950s buses from many of Britain's largest cities added variety to the A1 Service fleet. FOP 475 was a Daimler CWA6D with Park Royal bodywork built to the Ministry of Supply "wartime utility" specification although it was only delivered to Birmingham City Transport in 1946. Young Brothers of Galston purchased it in November 1949 and it is seen here on the Ardrossan stance in March 1953 with a former Glasgow Corporation Transport AEC Regent owned by Murray in the background.
Roy Marshall

When second hand vehicles have been purchased for A1 Service use they have usually been repainted into the fleet livery before being used. Few exceptions to this rule come to mind but one was EF 8108, an AEC Regal with Duple coachwork which was acquired by Kerr and Linney from Beeline of West Hartlepool. This view shows the vehicle at Parkhouse Road, Ardrossan in June 1950, shortly after purchase. Parkhouse Garage, owned at that time by Thomas Docherty, can be seen in the background.
A. B. Cross

In 1950 James Brown of Corsehill Garage, Springside acquired the share originally held by William Hill of Dreghorn and very soon afterwards this Weymann bodied Guy Arab was placed in service by the new owner. Initially, GTV 823 ran in the green livery of its previous owner, Skill and Son of Nottingham but by the time this photograph was taken it had been repainted into blue, white and maroon, and Brown had moved to Townfoot Garage, Dreghorn; reconstruction of that garage can be seen to be in progress behind the bus.
Roy Marshall

Nearly new buses which have been used by manufacturers for demonstration purposes have always been popular with A1 Service members on the lookout for bargains. Having purchased two similar buses in 1968/69, T. & E. Docherty took the opportunity to acquire the former Leyland Atlantean demonstrator MTF 665G in 1971, when it was just over two years old. The Park Royal dual-door bodywork had seating for 79 passengers and incorporated an illuminated advert panel on the offside, put to good use to advertise Docherty's separate coach fleet as shown by this August 1971 view in Princes Street, Ardrossan.
B. T. Deans

Hunter of Kilmarnock was the owner of UJF 181, a 1959 Daimler CSG6/30 with Metro-Cammell 74-seat rear entrance bodywork with platform doors and originally in the Leicester City Transport fleet. Acquired by Hunter in April 1972, it was withdrawn from passenger service about four years later after it had been damaged by vandals, following which it was cut down to form a tow truck. This photograph shows the bus in October 1972 in Ardrossan Road, Saltcoats bound for Kilmarnock.
B. T. Deans

In 1977 Docherty acquired AML 88H, a 1970 AEC Swift with 42-seat dual doorway bodywork by Park Royal, for use on the Broomlands community route bus service which he had developed on his own on behalf of the company. Later, when this service had become part of the general cycle of A1 duties, this bus was used on a variety of services but could often be found providing free shoppers facilities for a Tesco supermarket in Stevenston. Its original owner, London Transport, had this bus for six or seven years but it survived in the A1 fleet for almost twice that length of time before being sold for preservation.
G. M. Heaney

At the end of 1973 Brown purchased OHS979, a Daimler CVG6 with Massey 61-seat bodywork which had been new to McGill's bus service of Barrhead in 1959. It entered service in the A1 fleet in January 1974 and two months later Brown had also put sister vehicle OHS980 to work. Electrically-operated platform doors had been fitted to these buses by Brown when they were purchased.
Harry Hay

The style of bus more normally associated with the Birmingham City Transport fleet was represented in A1 Service by a few Daimlers and Leylands with this design of Metro-Cammell bodywork. EOG 280 was one of a pair of 1939 Leyland Titan TD6c purchased by Tom Hunter of Kilmarnock in 1951 and seen in this view of Glasgow Street, Ardrossan halted at the major road of Princes Street (for those old enough to remember our traditional roadsigns). Priority at this junction has since been changed, with traffic in Princes Street now having to give way to that in Glasgow Street.
Don Morris

BGA 82 was a Weymann bodied Daimler COG6 new in 1937 to Glasgow Corporation Transport but acquired by James Brown in 1951 and numbered 11. It had left the fleet by the end of 1953 but is seen here passing the Central Bar in Glasgow Street, Ardrossan, an area which has been altered considerably by redevelopment.
S. N. J. White

In addition to Daimlers, surplus AEC and Albion buses from the Glasgow Corporation fleet were acquired by various members in the early 1950s. DGB 467 was one of a pair of Pickering bodied Albion Venturer CX19s operated by Hill and Paterson at that time. It was new in 1940 and arrived in the A1 fleet 13 years later via Millburn Motors, at that time a well-known dealer in buses based at Alexandra Parade in Glasgow.
Roy Marshall

In April 1954 the first of what was to become a flood of former London Transport buses joined the fleet. FJJ 760 was a 1939 AEC Regent with bodywork built by London Transport and numbered STL 2600 in the London fleet. Steele owned this bus in its A1 days, and this view of it in the St Marnock Street stance in Kilmarnock shows that it retained its roof-mounted route number box (a peculiarly London feature) at that time, although it was removed later.

Buses of Guy manufacture were well represented in the fleet in the 1950s but the only double deck bus of this make which was bought new was GSD 229, an Arab Mk IV with Northern Counties bodywork supplied to John Stewart and Sons of Saltcoats in April 1955. It gave stalwart service until 1972 and this photograph shows it at work in Stanley Road, Ardrossan.
R. H. G. Simpson

247 AJF was one of a trio of former Leicester City Transport Leyland Titan PD3As with Metro-Cammell rear entrance bodywork bought by A1 Service members in 1975. It was owned by J. C. Stewart of Stevenston and lasted in the fleet until late 1977; in this June 1976 photograph it is shown opposite Saltcoats railway station, where environmental improvement works have since changed the scene considerably.
S. Little

Following their premature withdrawal by London Transport, a number of Park Royal or Metro-Cammell bodied Leyland Fleetline FE30AGRs were snapped up by various A1 Service members from 1983 onwards, when these buses were only about seven years old. OUC 46R was a Metro-Cammell bodied example owned by Hunter of Dreghorn from May 1983, photographed while picking up passengers in Manse Street, Saltcoats at the stop known for years as "the studio", shortly after it entered service. KSD 62W, the Alexander bodied Leyland Atlantean behind, is one of McMenemy's buses.
G. M. Heaney

NTU 465, an early example of the underfloor engined AEC Regal Mk IV with centre-entrance Plaxton coachwork, was owned by Steele, having come from Moss and Smith of Macclesfield. Although the vehicle can be seen to have a destination screen, passengers at the St Marnock Street stance in Kilmarnock would not have been used to travelling on a coach like this in A1 Service.
A. J. Douglas

In 1949 London Transport took delivery of 120 AEC Regents with Cravens bodywork to a style which was significantly different from the other 4000-plus vehicles in the RT class of buses. This was no doubt a factor in the premature disposal of these buses and A1 Service members took advantage of the bargain by buying 25 of them in 1956/57, and two more later via other operators. JXC 208 was one of six owned by T. & J. Hunter of Kilmarnock and lasted until 1962 when it was broken up, but other vehicles of this type spent considerably more of their working lives in Ayrshire than in London.
J. Thomson

In 1956 several youthful Leyland Titan PD2s with either highbridge or lowbridge Leyland bodywork joined the fleet from the Lanarkshire company, Hutchison of Overtown. JVA 161 was one of the highbridge examples, as can be seen in this view taken in Glasgow Street, Ardrossan, and it was owned by Brown of Dreghorn from 1956 until 1973. Some time after it left the A1 Service fleet, this bus was acquired by a preservation group but its intended restoration did not work out and it was eventually scrapped. *Roy Marshall*

In 1957 four former Barrow Corporation Crossley DD42s with characteristic Crossley bodywork were acquired by A1 Service members, and at the same time five similar buses from the same source joined the neighbouring Clyde Coast fleet. EO 8656 was owned by William Stewart of Stevenston and is seen outside Eugene's Cafe in Princes Street, Ardrossan. *R. H. G. Simpson*

For a number of years many of the buses bought by Steele had started life with independently-owned firms in Yorkshire. Leyland Titan PD1 FWR 773 fell into this category, having come from Severn, a Doncaster based company, in 1958. It was also typical of Steele's purchases of that era in that it had Roe bodywork. Manse Street, Saltcoats is again the location of this photograph.
R. F. Mack

One of the most unusual looking double deck buses ever to run in A1 Service was BRN 283, a Leyland Titan PD1/3 with a Burlingham full-fronted body. When new, this bus was one of Ribble's "White Ladies" used on medium distance express services to and from the Lancashire coastal resorts but in 1960 it was acquired by member Young Bros, of Galston, although it changed hands the following year when Young's share was sold to McKinnon. This view shows the vehicle in Irvine Road, Kilmarnock.
A. J. Douglas

The London Transport RT class of AEC Regents ultimately numbered well over 4,500 vehicles, all but 150 of which were built after the Second World War. Two of the earliest batch delivered in 1939/40 found their way into the A1 Service fleet and FXT 233, owned by R. Meney and Son of Ardrossan, was one of them. It was purchased by that member in August 1960 and photographed in Sharphill Road, Saltcoats while operating on the Springvale service.
A. J. Douglas

In 1961 the only Bristol double deck buses ever used in A1 Service arrived in the shape of two 1946 K6A models with lowbridge Eastern Coach Works bodywork, previously owned by the large Crosville company. FFM 442 was operated by William Stewart of Stevenston and is seen in this view outside Ardrossan post office in that town's Glasgow Street, coincidentally bound for Stevenston Pillar Box.
Roy Marshall

Further interest was added to the fleet in the autumn of 1963 when a small batch of new buses with rare Strachans bodywork entered service with a selection of owners. At least one of these vehicles carried the incorrect "A1 Bus Service" fleetname when new. WCS 194 was an AEC Regent Mk V owned by R. Meney and Son, seen bound for Ardrossan in the section of Kilwinning Main Street which was pedestrianised following completion of the North Service Road some years ago.
Ian Maclean

Andrew Hunter of Dreghorn operated three of these former London Transport Leyland Titans with this one, LUC 305, being purchased in 1964 as a replacement for similar JXN 313 which had been acquired six years earlier, together with JXN 367. These buses had the Leyland nameplate at the top of the radiator grille replaced by a plate bearing the name Hunter, a useful aid in identifying which buses belonged to which owners. In this view of Manse Street, Saltcoats the bus is bound for Ardrossan, despite the destination displayed.
R. F. Mack

Few photographs appear to exist of this Alexander bodied Leyland Atlantean. Delivered in January 1968 to J. C. Stewart of Stevenston, JSD 939F had been built to the Glasgow Corporation Transport style of that time right down to the destination screen layout and the Leyland Albion Atlantean badges, which for some years had been fitted to Glasgow's Leyland intake as a sop to that city, no longer able to buy genuine Albions. This bus had a short life, though, as it was destroyed in a fire at Stewart's garage in November 1969. It is seen here in St Marnock Street, Kilmarnock.
A. J. Douglas

One of the last of the traditional style of London Transport buses to reach the A1 Service fleet was MLL 834, a 1952 AEC Regent with Weymann bodywork also owned by J. C. Stewart. This bus started life as London Transport RT 3524 and later saw service with Samuel Ledgard of Leeds, but when that company was acquired by the West Yorkshire Road Car Co. Ltd. in 1967 it was surplus to requirements. Stewart purchased it in March 1968 and ran it for three months on a private contract, still in Ledgard blue and grey livery, but thereafter it became a fully fledged member of the A1 Service fleet and remained in use until 1970.
Roy Marshall

At the beginning of 1970 a trio of former Edinburgh Corporation Transport Guy Arab Mk IVs with Alexander bodywork entered service with A1 members. NSF 902, owned by Hunter of Kilmarnock, has exchanged Princes Street, Edinburgh for the rather different Princes Street, Ardrossan in this view. An environmental improvement scheme has recently changed the appearance of the latter with planters along the centre of the street having successfully disguised its width.
Roy Marshall

In addition to the Guys, eight former Edinburgh Corporation Leyland Titan PD2s with Metro-Cammell Orion bodywork joined the fleet in 1970/71 in the ownership of various members. LFS 468 arrived in November 1970 and was one of a pair which belonged to J. J. Stewart of Saltcoats. In this view it is seen in Irvine High Street bound for Chapelhill Mount, Ardrossan, an area where bus service provision was only resolved by the Traffic Commissioner adjudicating between A1 Service and Western SMT claims.
Brian Coney Collection

In May 1972 two Leyland Atlanteans with Alexander bodywork were delivered to Claude Dunn of Stevenston and J. J. Stewart of Saltcoats and may have been the first buses supplied new with no maroon relief in their livery. WCS 831K was Stewart's bus and was photographed leaving Kilmarnock bus station, bound for Ardrossan, Chapelhill.
A. J. Douglas

Having taken delivery of batches of Daimler Fleetlines with Alexander AD-type lowbridge bodies in 1966 and 1970, the Alexander AL-type highbridge body on Leyland Atlantean or Daimler Fleetline chassis was favoured for bulk orders in the 1973-79 period, resulting in a fairly standardised intake of new buses at that time. Three Atlanteans and five Fleetlines with this style of body arrived in 1973, and OAG 756L was one of the former owned by J. C. Stewart of Stevenston. Many owners take the opportunity to advertise their other business interests on their buses, as illustrated in this view at the new Kilmarnock bus station in Green Street.
A. J. Douglas

The later batches of Fleetlines ordered by A1 Service members arrived as Leyland FE30AGRs, rather than Daimlers, as the latter name had been phased out by Leyland. ASD 28T is one of five delivered in the spring of 1979 with Alexander bodywork, this particular example being supplied to Murray of Saltcoats. When Murray retired from the company in 1982, his double share was split between Robert Meney and the Stevenston Motor Company, and this bus moved to the latter owner at that time.
J. G. Fender

Although located only a few miles from the factory producing front engined Ailsas, Andrew Hunter attempted in the late 1970s to purchase a front-engined Dennis Jubilant, a type which was being manufactured largely for the Hong Kong market. This individualistic attempt did not come to fruition, however, largely because of the difficulty in finding a coachbuilder willing to construct such a one-off vehicle for the home market and in the end a Dennis Dominator with East Lancs bodywork was ordered instead. ECS 58V was the result, seen here at the coachworks in Blackburn just before delivery in 1979.
Roy Marshall

Not long after the re-admittance of single deck buses to the fleet, the Leyland National made its appearance with the purchase of KCS 179W by Hunter of Kilmarnock in 1980. When new, it had dual-door bodywork but it was soon converted to single door layout. It was never a popular bus, however, and in 1985 it was sold to Dodds of Troon for further use in the AA Motors fleet. This view shows it picking up passengers in Irvine High Street, bound for Ardrossan.
Roy Marshall

Providing a sharp contrast with the Leyland National and illustrating the diversity of the A1 fleet, OSJ 1X is a Leyland Tiger with unusual stepped-waistrail Duple Dominant Express coachwork. It was supplied new to Brown in 1982 and throughout its life has been used on a mixture of private hire and service work. In this view at Irvine Courthouse it is bound for the Magnum leisure centre.
G. M. Heaney

In 1982 McKinnon took delivery of a pair of Leyland Tigers with Wadham Stringer Vanguard bodywork which incorporated coach seating, but by the time this photograph was taken at Crosshouse Hospital in summer 1991, OSJ 35X had been re-seated with a set of bus seats. This new hospital is well served by the buses of A1 Service as it lies on both the Ardrossan-Kilmarnock and the Irvine-Dundonald-Kilmarnock routes.
G. M. Heaney

In 1983 McMenemy purchased this Leyland Leopard with bus-seated Duple Dominant coach body principally for use on the services to and from Glasgow which were introduced in July of that year. MTV 753P was new to Nottingham City Transport in 1976 but in this view it is seen at Stevenston Cross bound for Glasgow in March 1989.
M. Currie

When deregulation of local bus services was introduced in 1986 several former Passenger Transport Executive bus operations in the English conurbations were reduced in size to trim costs, and many relatively youthful buses were offered for sale as a result. A1 Service members were not slow to take advantage of this and six Roe bodied Leyland Olympians from the West Yorkshire PTE fleet were acquired at that time. CUB 73Y, owned by Mrs Hunter of Dreghorn, is seen in Bank Street, Irvine which formed part of an alternative route to Irvine High Street when that street was pedestrianised on an experimental basis.
A. J. Douglas

A new make for the fleet appeared in 1986 when Brown purchased this East Lancs bodied Scania N112DR, although a demonstrator of the same combination had been tried the previous year. C100 HSJ, photographed in Dreghorn, turned out to be the first of two such vehicles for this owner, but the second example had a very short A1 Service career as it arrived in 1986 and left the fleet three years later. It is now owned by Nottingham City Transport but this bus soldiers on in Ayrshire.
G. M. Heaney

Volvo Citybus C101 CUL was an interesting purchase by McMenemy in February 1988. When supplied new to London Buses, this bus was fitted with an experimental Volvo Cumulo hydraulic accumulator drive system but this had been replaced by a normal transmission arrangement before it joined the A1 Service fleet. Its Alexander dual-door body incorporated an unusual split step height design in the front entrance, intended to assist infirm passengers. Despite its relative youth, it did not remain in the fleet for long and had been sold within a few months of this photograph being taken in Irvine High Street in October 1988.
M. Currie

Over the years many of the owners have run luxury coaches under the umbrella of the A1 Service operators licence as most do not have such a licence of their own. While Tom Hill's Stevenston Motor Company tends not to do this, several coaches were owned in the 1980s principally for use on the Glasgow services. Former Park's of Hamilton Plaxton Paramount bodied Volvo B10M-61 E575 UHS was one of them, entering service on 1 November 1988 on the Ardrossan/Glasgow route — the day on which this photograph was taken. It was, however, sold shortly after this owner withdrew from operating the Glasgow services at the beginning of September 1989.
G. M. Heaney

An unusual addition to the fleet in 1989 was this 1975 Leyland Atlantean, fitted with bodywork by Eastern Coach Works, distinguished in this design by the window arrangement at the front corners of the lower deck. JHK 500N had previously been in the Colchester Borough Transport fleet but when this photograph was taken at Saltcoats station it was owned by Hunter of Kilmarnock, although it passed into Docherty's ownership soon afterwards when Hunter sold out.
G. M. Heaney

In 1975 a trial batch of five Irvine built Ailsa B55-10 with Alexander bodywork was supplied to NBC subsidiary Maidstone and District. Several similar buses were bought new by A1 Service members, so not surprisingly when the Maidstone buses were for sale in 1983, some were bought by A1 owners. By 1985 all had returned to Ayrshire in A1 ownership. LKP 383P, owned by Hunter of Grosshouse, shows that owner's livery with a maroon band below the lower deck windows.
John Burnett

The 1991 Fleet

Representative of the vehicles being added to the fleet in A1's sixtieth year as a limited company is SDA 655S, a Leyland Fleetline FE30AGR with bodywork by Park Royal and previously owned by West Midlands Travel. Ten of these buses with either Park Royal or Metro-Cammell bodies had been purchased by various members by the summer of 1991, but this example is owned by Brown and seen in its new home town of Dreghorn. New school transport contracts in the Kilmarnock area prompted the purchase of the majority of these buses, and those in question are largely confined to this work.
G. M. Heaney

Registration	Chassis		Bodybuilder	Seating	New
J. Brown & Son, Dreghorn; 3 shares					
NCS 20P	Leyland Fleetline	FE30AGR	Alexander	H43/31F	1976
NCS 21P	Leyland Fleetline	FE30AGR	Alexander	H43/31F	1976
OJD 161R	Leyland Fleetline	FE30AGR	Park Royal	H45/32F	1977
OJD 162R	Leyland Fleetline	FE30AGR	Park Royal	H45/32F	1977
SDA 562S	Leyland Fleetline	FE30AGR	MCW	H43/33F	1978
SDA 655S	Leyland Fleetline	FE30AGR	Park Royal	H43/33F	1978
TVP 900S	Leyland Fleetline	FE30AGR	MCW	H43/33F	1978
WDA 664T	Leyland Fleetline	FE30AGR	Park Royal	H43/33F	1979
HSJ 61V	Leyland Atlantean	AN68B/1R	Roe	H43/32F	1980
OSJ 1X	Leyland Tiger	TRCTL11/2R	Duple	C53F	1982
C100 HSJ	Scania	N112DR	East Lancs	H47/33F	1986

T. & E. Docherty, Irvine; 3 shares

SCS 384M	Volvo	B58-56	Duple	C51F	1974
JHK 500N	Leyland Atlantean	AN68/1R	ECW	H43/31F	1975
NCS 25P	Ailsa	B55-10	Alexander	H44/35F	1976
NCS 26P	Leyland Leopard	PSU3C/4R	Duple	C51F	1976
NSP 331R	Ailsa	B55-10	Alexander	H44/31F	1976
NSP 332R	Ailsa	B55-10	Alexander	H44/31F	1976
NSP 333R	Ailsa	B55-10	Alexander	H44/31F	1976
NSP 334R	Ailsa	B55-10	Alexander	H44/31F	1976
NSP 335R	Ailsa	B55-10	Alexander	H44/31F	1976
UCS 896S	Ailsa	B55-10	Alexander	H44/35F	1978
AYR 322T	Leyland National	10351A/IR	Leyland	B36D	1979
ECS 56V	Ailsa	B55-10 Mk II	Alexander	H44/35F	1979
KMA 399T	Leyland National	11351A/1R	Leyland	B49F	1979
A308 RSU	Volvo Citybus	B10M-50	East Lancs	H47/36F	1983
TSD 285	Volvo Citybus	B10M-50	Alexander	H47/37F	1985

In addition, the following vehicles are in storage:

NTF 9	Leyland Titan	PD2/15	Leyland	H30/26R	1951
BHN 601B	Leyland Titan	PD3/2	Alexander	H41/31F	1959
LXS 14K	Leyland Atlantean	PDR1A/1	Alexander	H44/34F	1972
JGA 198N	Leyland Atlantean	AN68/1R	Alexander	H45/31F	1975

BHN 601B was originally registered TSD 285.

Parkhouse Garage, Ardrossan; 2 shares

NCS 18P	Leyland Fleetline	FE30AGR	Alexander	H43/31F	1976
NCS 19P	Leyland Fleetline	FE30AGR	Alexander	H43/31F	1976
XPK 41T	AEC Reliance	6U2R	Plaxton	C53F	1978
ASD 26T	Leyland Fleetline	FE30AGR	Alexander	H45/33F	1979
ASD 27T	Leyland Fleetline	FE30AGR	Alexander	H45/33F	1979
CUB 50Y	Leyland Olympian	ONLXB/1R	Roe	H47/29F	1982
OAG 765	Volvo	B10M-61	Plaxton	C53F	1987
F149 XCS	Leyland Olympian	ONCL10/1RZ	Leyland	H47/31F	1988
G569 ESD	Volvo	B10M-55	Plaxton	B55F	1990

OAG 765 was originally registered D812 SGB. Neither of the coaches is in A1 livery.

Four out of the five Leyland Olympians supplied to members in 1989 had Leyland bodywork, but F747 XCS was the odd man out in having Alexander bodywork. This bus is owned by McMenemy and was purchased as a replacement for the Volvo Citybus C101CUL; this view shows it picking up passengers outside Brown's garage at Townfoot, Dreghorn.
G. M. Heaney

A. Hunter, Dreghorn; 1 share

CUB 72Y	Leyland Olympian	ONLXB/1R	Roe	H47/29F	1983
CUB 73Y	Leyland Olympian	ONLXB/1R	Roe	H47/29F	1983
EWY 74Y	Leyland Olympian	ONLXB/1R	Roe	H47/29F	1983
F41 XCS	Leyland Olympian	ONCL10/1RZ	Leyland	H47/31F	1989

J. McKinnon, Kilmarnock; 2 shares

KON 336P	Daimler Fleetline	FE30AGR	MCW	H43/33F	1976
NOC 380R	Daimler Fleetline	FE30AGR	MCW	H43/33F	1976
OCS 114R	Daimler Fleetline	CRG6LXB	Alexander	H44/31F	1976
NOC 450R	Daimler Fleetline	FE30AGR	MCW	H43/33F	1977
NOC 458R	Daimler Fleetline	FE30AGR	MCW	H43/33F	1977
OJD 214R	Leyland Fleetline	FE30AGR	MCW	H45/32F	1977
WDA 914T	Leyland Fleetline	FE30AGR	MCW	H43/33F	1978
ASD 29T	Leyland Fleetline	FE30AGR	Alexander	H45/33F	1979
DWH 700W	Leyland Fleetline	FE30AGR	Northern Counties	H43/32F	1980
OSJ 35X	Leyland Tiger	TRBTL11/2R	Wadham Stringer	B49F	1982
OSJ 36X	Leyland Tiger	TRBTL11/2R	Wadham Stringer	B49F	1982

J. McMenemy, Ardrossan; 1 share

MTV 753P	Leyland Leopard	PSU3C/4R	Duple	B53F	1976
NOC 407R	Daimler Fleetline	FE30AGR	MCW	H43/33F	1976
KSD 62W	Leyland Atlantean	AN68B/1R	Alexander	H45/33F	1980
A93 PKJ	Volvo	B10M-61	Duple	C48Ft	1983
F747 XCS	Leyland Olympian	ONCL10/1RZ	Alexander	H47/32F	1989

A93 PKJ is not in A1 livery

R. Meney & Son, Saltcoats; 3 shares

NCS 11P	Leyland Fleetline	FE30AGR	Alexander	H43/31F	1976
NCS 15P	Leyland Atlantean	AN68A/1R	Alexander	H43/31F	1976
NCS 17P	Leyland Fleetline	FE30AGR	Alexander	H43/31F	1976
NSP 336R	Ailsa	B55-10	Alexander	H44/31D	1976
NSP 338R	Ailsa	B55-10	Alexander	H44/31D	1976
ASD 25T	Leyland Fleetline	FE30AGR	Alexander	H45/33F	1979
ASD 30T	Leyland Atlantean	AN68A/1R	Alexander	H45/33F	1979
EWY 75Y	Leyland Olympian	ONLXB/1R	Roe	H47/29F	1983
EWY 76Y	Leyland Olympian	ONLXB/1R	Roe	H47/29F	1983
B24 CGA	Volvo Citybus	B10M-50	Alexander	H47/37F	1985
G164 ECS	Volvo	B10M-60	Van Hool	C51Ft	1989
G165 ECS	Volvo	B10M-60	Van Hool	C51Ft	1989

None of the coaches are in A1 livery.

R. B. Steele, Stevenston; 1 share

UCS 186S	Ailsa	B55-10	Alexander	H44/31D	1978
HGD 213T	Leyland Atlantean	AN68/1R	Alexander	H45/33F	1978
DSD 55V	Leyland Atlantean	AN68A/1R	Roe	H43/34F	1979
GHS 215X	Fiat	60F10	Caetano	C18F	1981
B312 UNB	Volvo	B10M-61	Van Hool	C53F	1985
F680 LGG	Toyota Coaster	HB30	Caetano	C21F	1988

None of the coaches is in A1 livery.

DSD 55V, a Leyland Atlantean delivered to Steele in 1979, continues that owner's association with Roe bodywork which stretches back more than thirty years. Since the sale of the Hunter of Crosshouse shares to other owners in 1990, Steele's unit has been the last bastion of the traditional A1 livery with maroon relief. This photograph was taken in High Street, Irvine.
G. M. Heaney

Stevenston Motor Company; 2 shares

LKP 384P	Ailsa	B55-10	Alexander	H44/35F	1975
NCS 16P	Leyland Fleetline	FE30AGR	Alexander	H43/31F	1976
ASD 28T	Leyland Fleetline	FE30AGR	Alexander	H45/33F	1979
ASD 32T	Ailsa	B55-10 Mk II	Alexander	H44/35F	1979
C800 HCS	Leyland Olympian	ONLXB/1R	ECW	H45/32F	1986
F524 WSJ	Leyland Olympian	ONCL10/1RZ	Leyland	H47/31F	1988

J. Stewart, Stevenston; 3 shares

LKP 381P	Ailsa	B55-10	Alexander	H44/35F	1975
NCS 13P	Leyland Atlantean	AN68A/1R	Alexander	H43/31F	1976
TSD 163S	Leyland Atlantean	AN68A/1R	Roe	H43/33R	1977
ASD 31T	Leyland Atlantean	AN68A/1R	Alexander	H45/33F	1979
ECS 57V	Ailsa	B55-10 Mk II	Alexander	H44/35F	1979
JKW 310W	Leyland Atlantean	AN68B/1R	Marshall	H45/29D	1981
JKW 322W	Leyland Atlantean	AN68B/1R	Marshall	H45/29D	1981
JKW 335W	Leyland Atlantean	AN68B/1R	Marshall	H45/29D	1981
KSD 2W	Leyland Leopard	PSU3F/4R	Duple	C53F	1981

A1 Service, Ardrossan (i.e. company owned)

G575 YTR	Iveco Dailybus	49.10	Phoenix	B25F	1990
G576 YTR	Iveco Dailybus	49.10	Phoenix	B25F	1990

Note

The abbreviations used under "Seating" in these lists indicate the following: B, single deck bus; C, coach; D, dual door, i.e. at front and centre; F, front entrance; H, double deck bus; R, rear entrance; t, toilet. The actual seating capacity is shown in the form upper deck/lower deck where appropriate.

A notable milestone in A1 Service history was reached in July 1990 when the first buses owned by the company, rather than by the individual members, entered service. The vehicles in question were two Iveco-Ford minibuses with Phoenix bodywork including G575 YTR, seen here in North Service Road, Kilwinning. The purpose of their acquisition was to allow the introduction of two minibus routes on a trial basis, but to spread the commercial risk involved in their experimental operation between all of the members.
G. M. Heaney

Further variety was added to the A1 Service fleet in the summer of 1991 when Stewart of Stevenston acquired a trio of Leyland Atlanteans with unusual bodywork built by Marshall of Cambridge. These dual-door buses started life in 1981 with the South Yorkshire Passenger Transport Executive and JKW 322W illustrates the type in this view at Parkhouse Road stance, Ardrossan soon after they were purchased.
D. J. Little

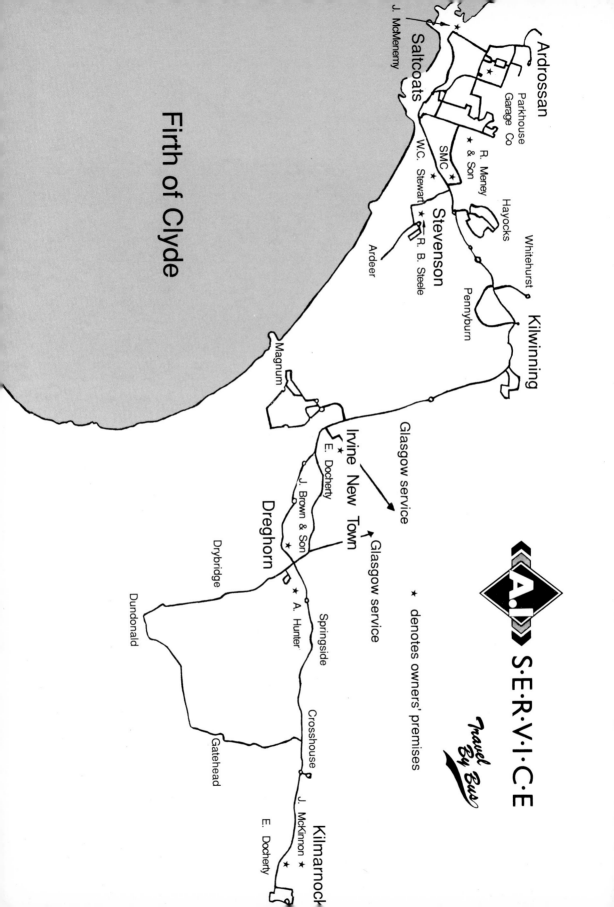